But in the beginning,
at the time of creation,
"God made them male and female,"
as the scripture says.
". . . and the two will become one."
So they are no longer two, but one.
—Mark 10:6, 8, TEV

For

_____

and

_____

May this book serve to strengthen
the bond of love
that already exists between you.

From

_____

When You Are Getting Married

RON DELBENE

with

MARY & HERB MONTGOMERY

UPPER ROOM BOOKS

NASHVILLE

The Upper Room Web site: www.upperroom. org

This booklet is part of a series of resources that also includes: *When an Aging Loved One Needs Care, When Your Child Is Baptized, and When You Are Facing Surgery.*

Cover and Book Design: Nelson Kane
Book Design: Jim Bateman
First Printing: April 1991 (10)
Second Printing: November 1997 (4)

ISBN: 0-8358-0637-5

Printed in the United States of America

Contents

Marriage is an opportunity to satisfy the yearning many people have for a special closeness with another person. It is a chance both to give and receive love. But making the love that first attracted you to one another grow into something deep and enduring takes time, patience, and the will to make it happen.

Although many factors influence a marriage, in the end, it is the two of you—a new couple—who determine the quality of your life together. Making the most of marriage means making the most of yourselves as persons. When you help one another do that, you come to a new understanding of the promises that you make to one another before God on your wedding day.

May reading this book give you insights that help you better understand yourselves and the expectations you each have for marriage.

Ron DelBene

Editor's Note: The stories in this book are true. Personal names and some details have been changed to protect the privacy of individuals involved.

To love means to commit oneself without guarantee, to give oneself completely in the hope that our love will produce love in the loved person. Love is an act of faith.

—Erich Fromm
The Art of Loving

Communicating with Love

Let all that you do be done in love.
—1 Corinthians 16:14

Beth and Eric came to me to talk about their upcoming marriage. As Beth eagerly described plans for the wedding, I noticed Eric shooting doubtful glances at her. When I asked what was troubling him, he said, "We've had a total breakdown in communication about the kind of wedding we're going to have. Beth is planning an extravaganza. I just want something plain and simple. If we can't communicate about this, I'm wondering how we're going to deal with issues that come up after we're married."

Eric was right to be concerned. Inability to communicate is one of the most frequently mentioned causes for failed relationships. As long as two people keep talking *and* listening, the bond between them can grow stronger. Why was an elaborate wedding important to Beth? What was it about such a wedding that so troubled Eric? Only by discussing these questions and respecting each other's point of view could they arrive at a plan that would make them both happy with their wedding.

The better two people are able to express themselves, the greater their chances of having a marriage in which each partner feels respected and secure. True communication involves listening as well as talking. Communication allows each person to grow in knowledge of the other. It is important to remember, however, that a great deal of communicating is done with body language. Facial expressions, sighs, shrugs, and posture often express what we are feeling more accurately than do our words.

Admitting your true feelings takes courage, but making them known before and after marriage is worth the risk. When one partner speaks in a straightforward manner without being accusing, the other person may be encouraged to do the same. Each partner must also consider the other person instead of thinking only of himself or herself. The result is a constructive encounter instead of an angry scene. Even though there may be some tense moments, honest communication can clear up misunderstandings and improve your relationship. The bond between the two of you will continue to grow stronger if you make it a practice to communicate clearly and with love.

Use the following questions to help you begin talking about some important aspects of marriage.

- What do we hope to get from marriage?
- What do we feel we can give to marriage?
- What is our idea of an ideal marriage?

Friendship and the Two of Us

Encourage one another
and build up each other.
—1 Thessalonians 5:11

"I didn't think of Clark as a friend when I married him five years ago," Sheila said, "but if you were to ask me who my best friend is now, I wouldn't hesitate a moment. It's Clark for sure."

During her months of dating, Sheila was so consumed by romantic feelings for Clark that friendship wasn't something she gave much thought to. For many people, becoming friends after marriage, as Sheila and Clark did, is an unexpected bonus. Others who marry a close friend find romance growing with time. Either way, being friends increases the joy of marriage. A card sent for no particular reason, a shared joke, a note of apology left on a pillow—these and all the other caring actions woven into the fabric of daily living strengthen the bond of friendship as well as the bond of love.

A key to building friendship is the use of leisure time. Sharing interests—whether it is reading, bicycling, watching sporting events, or going for walks—helps two people become friends. As time passes, interests change and you will want to find new activities to enjoy together.

Friends want what is best for each other. Friendship in marriage includes trust and the freedom to grow as individuals. Because no one person can satisfy all of another person's needs, it is important to keep old friends and make new ones as well. As long as the commitment to your marriage comes first, having friends your partner doesn't share can strengthen, not weaken, your bond. At its best, marriage is a friendship between two people who cherish one another. How wonderful it is to discover, as Sheila did, that the person you married is also your very best friend.

List five words that best describe a friend.

His List   **Her List**

_____   _____

_____   _____

_____   _____

_____   _____

_____   _____

- Do you think of the person you are about to marry as a friend? Why or why not?
- What interests do you share?
- Are there interests you would like to develop that you could share?
- What are some things you enjoy doing by yourself or with someone other than the person you are going to marry?
- I have (a lot of, a few, enough, no good) friends.
- My best friend is my best friend because . . .

Part of a New Family

Love one another as I have loved you.
—John 15:12

More than twenty years have passed since I first met my wife's family, but I still remember how nervous I felt. I was raised as an only child, while Eleanor grew up with four brothers and one sister. During our dating days, those were just facts about our individual histories. After we became engaged, however, those facts became real people whose approval I wanted very much. The day Eleanor and I flew to St. Louis so I could meet her family, my stomach knotted itself long before the plane touched down. I met her mother first. Then, over a long, hot afternoon, I met Eleanor's brothers and sister one by one, and finally her father came home from work and I met him. All the while the knot in my stomach pulled tighter and tighter.

As an only child, I dreamed about being part of a large family, but relating to all those people at the family dinner table left me very ill at ease. I became even more uneasy when I discovered I was marrying into what I call "The Missouri Athletic Club." Athletics were not a high priority in my growing up years, but every time Eleanor's family got together, the emphasis was on sports. I especially remember the time we arrived for a visit and found the family tennis tournament sign-up sheet posted inside the front door. It was one of the many times in those early years when I felt embarrassed and inadequate.

Maybe you are marrying someone whose family you knew even before you began dating. Or, like me, you met the family after you fell in love. Whatever the case, you each come to marriage with a family your partner will become a part of. Getting to know that other family and finding your place in it is important to your future happiness.

Many couples enjoy getting to know one another and their families by looking through photo albums. If you don't have a family album, at least share some pictures of your babyhood and growing up years. It is also interesting and fun to look through your high school yearbooks. Sharing information, insights, and feelings is yet another way to learn about each other's family. Use the following exercise to get you started talking.

List five words you use to describe your families.

His List   **Her List**

_____   _____

_____   _____

_____   _____

_____   _____

_____   _____

- Some special (funny, unusual, or odd) things about my family that you need to know are . . .
- Some things that make me uneasy about meeting or being with your family are . . .

It is individuals, capable of loving and being loved, who can truly build a marriage. Their marriage will not absorb their individuality, nor destroy their individual goals, nor push them into artificial roles. They will know that only by being themselves can they relate to each other.

—Everett Shostrom and James Kavanaugh
Between Man and Woman

Constructive Conflict

Do not let the sun go down on your anger.
—Ephesians 4:26

Connie told me that the first time she and Tim had a fight she went to the bedroom and began throwing skirts and blouses in her suitcase. She thought the marriage was over! Connie reacted this way because she grew up in a household where she never saw marital conflict. Her father died when she was a toddler and her mother never remarried, so she did not understand that fights between husband and wife do not spell the end of a marriage. If handled properly, they can lead to an improved relationship.

Two people sharing their lives in a relationship as intimate as marriage will naturally experience some conflict. Situations arise that cause anger, resentment, jealousy. You may be tempted to suppress what you feel in order to maintain harmony, but doing so only puts up a wall between you. If the pattern of ignoring problems and denying feelings continues, the wall grows higher.

Instead of building walls, face problems and settle conflicts as they arise. Although confrontation may be painful, it indicates that two people care enough to face their problems and work on them. Constructive conflict can be an emotional housecleaning that leads to greater trust and understanding.

Discuss conflict as it relates to you and your relationship by sharing responses to the following questions.

- What have we disagreed about while dating?
- What do we see as potential areas of conflict after we are married?
- What steps can we take now to keep these issues from causing difficulties in our marriage?

Guidelines for Handling Conflict

1. **Choose an appropriate time and place.** A disagreement in front of others, or one begun the moment a person comes home, is off to a bad start.

2. **Describe your feelings instead of accusing the other person.** It is far less threatening to the other person's ego to hear the words, "I feel rejected when . . ." than to be told, "You make me feel rejected when you . . ."

3. **Express feelings as calmly as possible.** Hysteria and tears can be emotional blackmail.

4. **Stick to the subject.** If the disagreement is about overspending, don't introduce other issues.

5. **Appreciate the other person's right to a different point of view.** At the time of conflict this can be difficult, but when emotions cool, you may see things differently.

6. **Avoid words like "always" and "never."** A person who is told, "You're always late" or "You're never thoughtful" feels threatened and gets defensive. Focus shifts from solving the problem to defending oneself.

7. **Don't criticize in ways that hurt the other person's self-esteem.** Pointing out past failures or a physical feature about which the other person is sensitive is destructive and defeating to both partners.

8. **Never resort to physical violence.** Once unleashed, there is no telling where abuse will stop.

9. **Know when to end a quarrel.** Sometimes a disagreement needs to be ended before it is resolved. You may have to agree to disagree and take up the matter at another time. It is far better to do this than to accept an unsatisfactory solution.

Managing the Money

Having gifts that differ . . . , let us use them.
—Romans 12:6, RSV

By the time Vicki and Dan came to see me, money was causing a great deal of stress in their year-old marriage. "In my growing up years, my parents paid the bills first," Dan said. "Then if there was any money left over, we ate."

Vicki explained that in her family it was just the opposite. "We spent first; then we paid the most demanding creditors." She shook her head. "When you think about our different backgrounds, I guess it's not surprising that we have so many disagreements about money."

Psychologists say that while children are still toddlers, their parents' actions and feelings about money form the child's attitudes toward it. That does not mean you will duplicate your parents' spending habits, but their attitudes toward money will have an effect on you.

Whenever *your* money and *my* money become *our* money—as is so often the case in marriage—the potential for conflict is great. That potential is so great that many counselors rate disagreements over money as the leading cause of divorce. The problem may arise over the amount of money people have, but more often the trouble comes from failure to agree on how money should be spent.

Money has different meanings for each of us. To one, it may mean security or power. To the other, it might be independence or achievement. For almost all of us, money is status. When two people discuss what money means to them personally, it is no longer a mystery why one prefers a flashy boat to a savings account or a luxury car to an economy model. Understanding your attitudes toward money can open the door to making decisions about spending that you both agree on.

Every couple needs some method of money management. The following questions will help you see what needs to be discussed in order to make money a source of satisfaction instead of a cause for conflict.

- What is our total monthly take-home pay?
- What are our total monthly expenses?
- Will money be *yours* and *mine*, or *ours?*
- What did we learn from our parents about spending? about saving?
- Which of us is more willing and better qualified to handle money?
- What could we both do to become better money managers?
- How will we handle outstanding bills (credit card balances, other loan payments)?

Your History of Touch

"In our family we were huggers and touchers," George said. "I can't remember leaving the house a single morning without a kiss from my mom and a hug from my dad. I'm twenty-four now, and it's still that way when I go for a visit. But it sure is different when we go to Paula's place."

I looked at the petite young woman whom George was going to marry in a month and asked, "How was it for you, Paula?"

"George and I've tried to talk about this before, and it's really hard," she said. "I think his parents are wonderful people, but I absolutely shrink when they hug and kiss me. It's something I'm just not used to." She looked at her hands and paused for a long moment. "I've never mentioned this before, but my father was abusive, and that's why my mother divorced him. I know this is hard for George to understand, but even though I think it's great that his parents are touchers, it scares me. Even sometimes when George gets a little rough in a playful way, I think about the beatings my father gave Mom and me."

George was suddenly wide-eyed. "So that's why," he murmured more to himself than to Paula and me.

The three of us had a lot more talking to do. Although Paula and George had revealed some things about themselves, they needed to explore what effect their experiences of touch might have on their lovemaking.

Hank and Susan were another young couple who came to me before their wedding. In their case, Hank was the one who came from the nontouching family. "I can't ever remember my mother and father touching me except maybe when I was sick," he said. "I guess that's why I yearn so much for Susan to touch me, but I'm not certain how to ask for it. I know she feels that I touch her a lot just to get touched back. We talked about that once, but I didn't know how to say what I was feeling."

"It was very different in my family," Susan said, "especially with my dad. He's a really huggy kind of guy, so I love to have Hank hug me. I guess I'm going to have to learn to initiate some of the touching."

You, too, come to marriage with a history of touch. Sharing that history will give you a better understanding of each other's need and desire for touch.

For each of the following phrases, circle a number between 1 and 10 that indicates where you see yourself on the scale.

• As I was growing up, my experience of gentle, loving touch from my mother was:

(none 1 2 3 4 5 6 7 8 9 10 very satisfying)

• As I was growing up, my experience of gentle, loving touch from a significant other woman was:

(none 1 2 3 4 5 6 7 8 9 10 very satisfying)

• As I was growing up, my experience of gentle, loving touch from my father was:

(none 1 2 3 4 5 6 7 8 9 10 very satisfying)

• As I was growing up, my experience of gentle, loving touch from a significant other man was:

(none 1 2 3 4 5 6 7 8 9 10 very satisfying)

• My desire to touch people I care for is:

(nonexistent 1 2 3 4 5 6 7 8 9 10 very high)

• When people touch me as a gesture of affection, I am:

(uncomfortable 1 2 3 4 5 6 7 8 9 10 comfortable)

• Something about my history of touch that I think is important for you to know is . . .

More than Sex

Above all clothe yourselves with love,
which binds everything together
in perfect harmony.
—Colossians 3:14

"Sex itself isn't as big a part of being married as I thought it would be," said Caroline one year after her wedding. "I mean, how much time out of a busy life can you actually spend in bed?"

Caroline and I went on to talk about how sharing and intimacy in marriage involve so much more than a particular sex act. In a satisfying marriage, each partner has a feeling of emotional closeness that the other nurtures by being trustworthy and thoughtful. Lovemaking is that exciting extra dimension that enriches and enlivens married life. It is the most intimate way we have of expressing our love; it is the way God has given us to create new life.

Being comfortable with your sexuality is important in developing a healthy, happy sex life. Attitudes toward sex are learned, and any feelings that keep you from full participation in lovemaking can be unlearned and replaced by new attitudes. If sexual incompatibility or some other problem with sex causes ongoing strife in your marriage, it is wise to go to a qualified therapist. Marriage partners who openly face their problems usually overcome them with a little help from a skilled professional. Also, many good books and tapes are available on the subject of sexual fulfillment.

God has given us the pleasure of sex to bind us in married love and to let us share in the power of creation. Although sexual techniques can be mastered, in and of themselves they do not lead to a fulfilling sex life. It is the caring and tenderness of lovemaking that makes sex emotionally satisfying and gives it a spiritual dimension.

What truly determines the overall happiness of a marriage is your emotional life as a couple. Use the following questions to gain insights that will help you build a marriage in which you both find the fulfillment you seek.

- Can we express our feelings to one another?
- Do we resolve our differences before they become major problems?
- Can I ask my partner for what I desire?
- Am I willing to listen to my partner's desires?

Know *who you are singly and who you are as a couple. Know . . . what your strengths and your weaknesses are, what you have to offer, and what a child would simply have to tolerate. Self-awareness is the best, most reliable way to reach the final decision about whether or not you would like to be a parent.*

—Dr. Elizabeth M. Whelan
A Baby? . . . Maybe

Deciding about Parenthood

Guide me with your counsel.
—Psalm 73:24

Once married, the two of you will be a family. If either of you already has children, your family enlarges immediately. But the question of whether or not to have children of your own remains. You hear arguments for and against parenthood from friends, relatives, the church, and a society that tends to expect a young couple to have children.

The better you understand yourselves as individuals and as a couple, the more likely you are to make a wise decision about parenthood. Not everyone wants children, and some people should not have them. If it is your choice not to be parents, you should not allow anyone to make you feel guilty. If you are entering marriage with a baby already on the way, your relationship will require careful tending during the pregnancy and after the birth when you are new to both marriage and parenthood.

No matter when a birth occurs, a child puts strains on a marriage. But when you choose to meet the challenges of parenthood with love and mutual commitment, the marriage bond is strengthened because of the God-given life you have created together.

Sharing your answers to the following questions can help clarify your feelings about parenthood.

- What are your reasons for wanting or not wanting to be a parent?
- Have you considered that raising a child involves at least eighteen years of your life?
- If you have a child right away, will you be able to meet the financial obligations?
- Would a baby cause conflicts over careers?
- Are you both prepared to love a child, even if that child has physical or mental problems?
- What would be your hopes for a child?

Traditions You Bring to Marriage

*For where your treasure is,
there your heart will be also.*
—Luke 12:34

When I asked Melissa what was troubling her, she told me, "My birthday was last month. And when I mentioned to my coworkers that it was approaching, one of them said, 'Forget about getting anything just for you. From now on you'll be getting *we* gifts.'"

Although Melissa said she laughed along with everyone else in her office, she was thinking, Other men might do that, but not Stan! She went on to tell how, on the night of her birthday, her husband presented her with a large package with a red bow on top. Happy and excited, she opened it and found her very own VCR—something she and Stan had talked about getting for themselves someday. "I was crushed," Melissa said, "here it was my *first* birthday as Stan's wife, and I got a *we* gift!"

When I asked how birthdays were celebrated in her family, Melissa explained that it was their custom to give a bunch of little presents and one medium-size gift. "We were at my mom's house for supper on my birthday last year," she said. "After we sang 'Happy Birthday' and I blew out the candles, Mom and my sister brought out the presents. I bet there were ten little ones all wrapped up. There was a can of hair spray, a little travel sewing kit—not expensive things, but each one was wrapped as though it were a diamond ring. I opened every one before I got to the main gift, which was a sweater I had seen on a shopping trip with my sister."

"Were you ever at Stan's house for one of his birthdays?" I asked.

A puzzled, then knowing look came over Melissa's face. "I've been there two or three times. It was always just a regular meal with no cake or anything. After dinner there was one gift—and I mean a *big* gift. Usually it was an expensive coat or suit or something like that."

26

I nodded in recognition of a familiar situation. "You two grew up with very different traditions."

"*Very!*" Melissa agreed.

Through repeated ways of doing things, traditions emerge that make families unique. For one family it is not Christmas without placing an angel on top of the tree and opening gifts on Christmas Eve. For another family, the tradition is opening gifts on Christmas morning and going to church together.

Although we tend to associate traditions with the celebration of holidays and other special occasions, they are also part of the everyday aspects of family living. It might be a family tradition to have waffles for Sunday breakfast or to say grace before meals or to vacation at the same resort every summer. Each of you has your own background of traditions that you bring to marriage. When both backgrounds are taken into account and respected, new traditions will emerge that reflect who you are as individuals and as a couple.

To better understand the traditions you each bring to marriage, complete the following statements and share your responses.

- In our family we celebrated birthdays by . . .
- Christmas wouldn't be Christmas without . . .
- Some traditions in my family other than those on birthdays or at Christmas were . . .
- Some traditions from my background that I would like to bring to our marriage are . . .

In the Presence of God

And so I prayed,
and understanding was given me.
—Wisdom 7:7, JB

Because you are choosing to be married in a religious ceremony, you are acknowledging that God has a place in your life. Yet I am often met with embarrassed silence when I ask couples, "Do you ever pray together?"

When I asked Stephanie and Paul this question, Paul said, "We pray together in church, but that's about it."

I told this young couple that although their prayers in church were a good beginning, they needed to exercise their prayer life in order to grow spiritually. I suggested that as a start toward spiritual closeness, they each take time daily—maybe at bedtime, upon awakening, or whenever they looked at themselves in the mirror—to thank God for the gift of one another and for their relationship.

Ideally, a couple's prayer life becomes more intimate over time. They rely less on formal prayers and more on informal prayers in which they share with one another and with God what is on their minds and in their hearts. To me it is ironic that married people open their very bodies to one another but hesitate to share themselves in prayer because that is too personal. We are always in the presence of God, and couples who use prayer to unite themselves with one another and with God are in that presence in a very special way.

Wherever you are in your prayer life, sharing responses to the following questions will help you explore the spiritual dimension of your lives both as individuals and as a couple.

- What is your favorite part of—or the story you remember most vividly from—the Old Testament?
- What is your favorite part of—or the story you remember most vividly from—the New Testament?

- What was your family's prayer life like when you were growing up? Did you pray before meals? at bedtime? during times of crisis? at other times?
- Why is or isn't prayer an important part of your life?
- What are your prayer habits?
- Was there ever a time when you felt that you lost your faith and stopped praying?
- Was there ever a time when you were especially aware of God's presence?
- What part would you like prayer to have in your marriage?

Growing in Love

Above all,
maintain constant love for one another.
—1 Peter 4:8

"Ben and I have had a lot of struggles in the ten years we've been married," Janice told me, "but the love I feel for him now is much deeper than it was on our wedding day. I guess you could say that what we had back then was the appetizer. What we have together now is the main course."

Couples who grow in love also grow in intimacy. Having a warm and intimate marriage requires that you be open with one another, revealing your longings, your fears, your hopes, your dreams. It is well to remember, however, that we each differ in our capacity and desire for closeness. Maybe you feel a physical but not a spiritual closeness or an emotional but not an intellectual closeness. Feeling close in one area of your relationship gives hope that greater intimacy is possible in other areas as well. Trying to force closeness can bring discord, whereas patience and respect for the privacy of the other creates a climate of trust in which intimacy grows.

Marital closeness can be achieved only if you create time and space for one another. As you settle into married life, it is easy to let jobs, social commitments, sports, and membership in organizations not only consume your energy but rob you of time together. Whenever outside demands keep you from meeting each other's needs, you need to examine your life and reorganize your priorities.

Some couples find that it works well to plan a special time out together once a month on the anniversary date of their wedding. It doesn't matter if you eat at a fancy restaurant, stop for fast food, or have a picnic in the park. The important thing is that you do something with one another on a day that has meaning just for the two of you.

Every marriage has times when partners feel their needs are not being met, times when it appears easier to end the relationship than to work on its problems. That is when couples need to hold fast to their commitment and have faith that God is there for them. By being attentive to God's presence, you will have the courage to face your problems with the hope that when you overcome them, your marriage will be strengthened.

Satisfying marriages don't just happen, they develop. A happy, life-long marriage takes a great deal of understanding and consideration and a willingness to meet in the middle. Partners who grow in love make it a practice to communicate their feelings and bring their dreams up to date. In times of happiness, they celebrate their joy; in times of pain, they share the hurt. Over the years they discover—as you will—the wonders that love can work.

Love changes and grows. . . .
The amount of love
generated in a good marriage
cannot be imagined
by the young couple
just starting out.

—Dr. Joyce Brothers
The Brothers System for
Liberated Love and Marriage

About the Authors

The Reverend Ron DelBene holds a Master's degree in theology from Marquette University and has done additional post-graduate work in education, psychology, and counseling. He has been Assistant Professor of Theology, Director of a Campus Ministry Center, National Consultant in Religion for an education division of CBS, and a parish rector.

An Episcopal priest, Ron is active in peace and justice issues and has worked with Cursillo, Walk to Emmaus, and Kairos, as well as with various denominational judicatories in retreat and spiritual formation work.

He is presently Executive for Program at St. Luke's Church, Birmingham, Alabama. With his wife, Eleanor, he directs The Hermitage, a place for persons to enter into solitude and prayer under their direction. He is also the author of *The Breath of Life, Hunger of the Heart, Alone with God,* and *Into the Light: A Simple Way to Pray with the Sick and the Dying.*

The DelBenes have two children, Paul and Anne, and live in Trussville, Alabama.

Mary and Herb Montgomery are full-time writers who have created numerous books and educational projects to help both children and adults grow in faith. The Montgomerys live in Minneapolis and are the parents of three children.